Sum of

Rising Out of Hatred
Eli Saslow

Conversation Starters

By Paul Adams
Book Habits

Please Note: This is an unofficial Conversation Starters guide. If you have not yet read the original work, you can purchase the original book here.

We hope you enjoy this complimentary guide from BookHabits. Our mission is to aid readers and reading groups with quality thought-provoking material to in the discovery and discussions on some of today's favorite books.

Bonus Downloads
Get Free Books with __Any Purchase__ of Conversation Starters!

Every purchase comes with a FREE download!

Add spice to any conversation
Never run out of things to say
Spend time with those you love

Get it Now

or Click Here.

Scan Your Phone

Tips for Using Conversation Starters:

EVERY GOOD BOOK CONTAINS A WORLD FAR DEEPER THAN the surface of its pages. Questions herein are designed to bring us beneath the surface of the page and invite us into the world that lives on. These questions can be used to:

- Foster a deeper understanding of the book
- Promote an atmosphere of discussion for groups
- Assist in the study of the book, either individually or corporately
- Explore unseen realms of the book as never seen before

Table of Contents

Introducing *Rising Out of Hatred*

ising Out of Hatred: The Awakening of a Former White Nationalist is a book written by Eli Saslow. It tells the story of how a white supremacist who was groomed to be the next generation leader of white supremacists turned his back on the movement.

Derek Black's father is the founder of Stormfront, the Internet's largest racist group. His godfather was the KKK Grand Wizard David Duke. When he grew older he created his own radio show which was regarded by the nationalist movement as their guiding light.

He then went to college at Florida's liberal arts school, New College where he met new friends and was exposed to ideas different from what he was exposed to at home. Being home-schooled in his younger years, all this was new to him. Some students learned about his white supremacist ties and activities and exposed him resulting to his being shunned at school. Few people attempted to befriend him, including a Jewish student leader who invited him to Shabbat dinners at home with his Jewish family, and a white girl who believed there is a nice person behind his racist veneer. His beliefs slowly changed. He no longer supported the view that immigrants should be deported back home. He started to support Black Lives Matter, affirmative action, and same-sex marriage. In one encounter he expressed revulsion for his father's views about George Zimmerman who killed an unarmed Trayvon Martin. He realized that he needed to publicly express his new views about racism. He wrote a letter to the Southern Poverty Law Center and admitted his previously harmful actions that perpetuated racism against people of color and of Jewish descent.

The author starts his account of Black's conversion with a report on the 2008 gathering among white nationalist leaders just after the election of America's first African American president. The gathering was held in Memphis attended by Duke, Klansmen, and Neo-Nazis. The nineteen-year-old Black was among those who issued a speech before the crowd. He said, "We can take the country back...the great intellectual move to save white people started today." The book gives a detailed portrait of the young Black as a racist. He once performed the song "The Monkey Who Became President" to console his fellow racists. He ran and won as committeeman in Palm Beach County, Florida using white victimhood for his platform. He believed that Abraham Lincoln was racist and that James Monroe, Thomas Jefferson, and other historical leaders were similarly against people of color. When he entered college, he continued his promotion of anti-Semitism and racism through his radio speeches, though he did this secretly. He became friends with Peruvians and Jewish students. His double life was exposed when a student who was doing research on his paper learned that Black is an active racist advocate and leader. Links to Black's speeches, articles, and radio show were posted on the internet for everybody to see and he became a controversial figure on campus. This did not deter Mike Long, a Jewish student leader from befriending him. Through Long, Black met Allison Gornick, who used to shun him but gradually saw a different person behind his racist cloak. "She thought he seemed quirky, gentle, and interesting..." the author writes. Saslow features Gornick as a prominent figure in Black's conversion. She challenged Black's narrow views about race which caused Black to reconsider his beliefs. Saslow shows how Black went through evasion and contradictions as he evolved in his views. He noted the talks between Black and Gornick which indicated how Black made small revisions to his beliefs, including his acknowledging that he respects people of different colors and that he is a white nationalist who needs to protect other whites as if they are an endangered species. Saslow notes the significant change in his beliefs, as in the time he said he is no longer against immigrants and their forced deportation, adding that "maybe gradual self-deportation...they would leave on their own." Black's struggle to cut ties from his racist past is noted in many other instances. A highlight in the book is one of the major turning points in his conversion. This is the time when he realized that his father's views have become unacceptable, like that of his support for George Zimmerman. Black was horrified also because it showed him "...a memory of his previous self" who made flawed arguments and expressed callousness, cruelty, and ignorance. "It seemed obvious to him that he needed to publicly condemn not only white nationalism but also his past life," Saslow writes. In writing his apology to the Southern Poverty Law Center, Black's words are quoted by Saslow: "It has become clear to me that white nationalism is not a movement of positive identity or of asserting cultural values...I can't support a movement that tells me I can't be a friend to whomever I wish or that other people's races require me to think about them in a certain way..."

The Washington Post review says the book looks at the disturbing "spread of extremism-- and how it is planted and cultivated in the fertile soil of American bigotry." The review praises Saslow's "vivid storytelling" which also shows that redemption is possible.

Bestselling author of *Dark Money* Jane Mayer says Saslow's skill at telling contemporary tales is matchless. His stories are "most improbable, humane, and riveting." Elisha Wiesel, chairman of the

WVN Elie Wiesel Award cites the beautiful book and admits to being changed by it. He says it is powerfully told and shows that the future is "right and promising" because of the outstanding souls told about in the book. Pulitzer Prize winner and bestselling author of Directorate S. and Ghost Wars say the book brims with insight. He believes Saslow wrote "an instant classic of narrative writing and reporting."

Rising Out of Hatred is authored by the Pulitzer Prize winner Eli Saslow. He is the author of *Ten Letters: The Stories Americans Tell Their President.*

Discussion Questions

"Get Ready to Enter a New World"

Tip: Begin with questions dealing with broader issues to ensure ample time for quality discussions. Read through all discussion questions before engaging.

~~~

question 1

Derek Black's father is the founder of Stormfront, the Internet's largest racist group. His godfather was the KKK Grand Wizard David Duke. When he grew older he created his own radio show which was regarded by the nationalist movement as their guiding light. How was his childhood like? How did his parents bring him up with racist beliefs?

~~~

~ ~ ~

question 2

He then went to college at Florida's liberal arts school, New College where he met new friends and was exposed to ideas different from what he was exposed to at home. Being home-schooled in his younger years, all this was new to him. Apart from his change in beliefs how else did college change him as a person? Why do you think college is a very influential period in a young person's life?

~ ~ ~

~~~

question 3

Some students learned about his white supremacist ties and activities and exposed him resulting to his being shunned at school. How did this affect him?

~~~

question 4

The author starts his account of Black's conversion with a report on the 2008 gathering among white nationalist leaders just after the election of America's first African American president. The gathering was held in Memphis attended by Duke, Klansmen, and Neo-Nazis. The nineteen-year-old Black was among those who issued a speech before the crowd. He said, "We can take the country back...the great intellectual move to save white people started today." Why do you think the author chose this part to open the book? What is it's significance?

question 5

The book gives a detailed portrait of the young Black as a racist. He once performed the song "The Monkey Who Became President" to console his fellow racists. He ran and won as committeeman in Palm Beach County, Florida using white victimhood for his platform. He believed that Abraham Lincoln was racist and that James Monroe, Thomas Jefferson, and other historical leaders were similarly against people of color. How do you feel about him being raised on the belief that Lincoln and Jefferson were racists?

~~~

question 6

Saslow depicted Don Black as a loving father. He showed that father and son had a strong bond. How do you think Derek felt when he decided to turn against his father's beliefs? How do you feel about a racist father who is entirely capable of loving his family?

~~~

~~~

question 7

When he entered college, he continued his promotion of anti-Semitism and racism through his radio speeches, though he did this secretly. He became friends with Peruvians and Jewish students. His double life was exposed when a student who was doing research on his paper learned that Black is an active racist advocate and leader. Links to Black's speeches, articles, and radio show were posted on the internet for everybody to see and he became a controversial figure on campus. This did not deter Mike Long, a Jewish student leader from befriending him. What did Mike Long think about befriending a racist? Why did he not shun Black like the others?

~~~

question 8

Through Long, Black met Allison Gornick, who used to shun him but gradually saw a different person behind his racist cloak. "She thought he seemed quirky, gentle, and interesting..." the author writes. Saslow features Gornick as a prominent figure in Black's conversion. She challenged Black's narrow views about race which caused Black to reconsider his beliefs. How was Gornick able to know Black better? What was her attitude upon meeting him?

~~~

question 9

Saslow shows how Black went through evasion
and contradictions as he evolved in his views. He
noted the talks between Black and Gornick which
indicated how Black made small revisions to his
beliefs, including his acknowledging that he
respects people of different colors and that he is a
white nationalist who needs to protect other
whites as if they are an endangered species. What
other kinds of evasion and self-contradiction did
he go through? Do you think he was aware of the
confusion that resulted in his contradictory
beliefs?

~~~

question 10

Saslow notes the significant change in his beliefs, as in the time he said he is no longer against immigrants and their forced deportation, adding that "maybe gradual self-deportation…they would leave on their own." What experiences led him to change his belief about immigrant deportation?

~~~

~~~

question 11

Black's struggle to cut ties from his racist past is noted in many other instances. A highlight in the book is one of the major turning points in his conversion. This is the time when he realized that his father's views have become unacceptable, like that of his support for George Zimmerman. Black was horrified also because it showed him "...a memory of his previous self" who made flawed arguments and expressed callousness, cruelty, and ignorance. How did his father react to his change of heart? How did his father regard him afterward?

~~~

~~~

question 12

"It seemed obvious to him that he needed to publicly condemn not only white nationalism but also his past life," Saslow writes. In writing his apology to the Southern Poverty Law Center, Black's words are quoted by Saslow: "It has become clear to me that white nationalism is not a movement of positive identity or of asserting cultural values...I can't support a movement that tells me I can't be a friend to whomever I wish or that other people's races require me to think about them in a certain way..." Why does he quote Black in this particular instance? What is the effect of Saslow quoting Black's own words?

~~~

~~~

question 13

Media critics say that Saslow wrote "an instant classic of narrative writing and reporting." What makes his book stand out as a narrative and reportage? Why do you think it is considered a classic?

~~~

~~~

question 14

Critics praise Saslow's "vivid storytelling." His book accordingly shows that redemption is possible. How does Black's story show that redemption is possible? How does this impact on the supremacist movement in general?

~~~

~~~

question 15

His beliefs slowly changed. He started to support Black Lives Matter, affirmative action, and same-sex marriage. What factors led to these changes in belief? Who are the people who enabled him to see the truth about black lives and same-sex marriage?

~~~

~~~

question 16

The Washington Post review says the book looks at the disturbing "spread of extremism-- and how it is planted and cultivated in the fertile soil of American bigotry." How has the book enlightened you about extremism and in America? Are you surprised by the things you learned? Why?

~~~

question 17

Bestselling author of Dark Money Jane Mayer says Saslow's skill at telling contemporary tales is matchless. His stories are "most improbable, humane, and riveting." What makes his stories humane and riveting? Why does Mayer say his stories are most improbable?

~~~

question 18

Elisha Wiesel, chairman of the WVN Elie Wiesel Award, cites the beautiful book and admits to being changed by it. He says it is powerfully told and shows that the future is "right and promising" because of the outstanding souls told about in the book. Does the book change you as well? In what way?

~~~

~~~

question 19

Pulitzer Prize winner and bestselling author of Directorate S. and Ghost Wars Steve Coll says the book brims with insight. What insights about racism and Black's story strike you the most in the book? Why?

~~~

question 20

Rising Out of Hatred is authored by the Pulitzer Prize winner Eli Saslow. He is the author of Ten Letters: The Stories Americans Tell Their President. Do you think this book merits another Pulitzer? Why? Why not?

~~~

Introducing the Author

Eli Saslow spent hundreds of hours talking to Derek Black in order to understand him and his conversion. He also interviewed his classmates at the New College in Florida, including those who refused to talk to him as well as those who engaged with him in discussions and debates. There were immigrant students and Jewish students who were also interviewed for the book. Saslow also interviewed people from the white nationalist movement, including Derek's family. He had access to Black's emails, g-chats, Facebook where Black held debates that promoted his racist beliefs. Saslow says he first learned about Black when he was writing a story about Dylann Roof who shot people in a Charleston church. He came across Stormfront, the website founded by Black's father. Roof spent a lot of time reading through the website and used their language in his personal manifesto. Saslow noticed the biggest thread in the website is about Derek Black, whose father and Stormfront founder Don Black talked about his son's leaving the movement. Saslow tried to reach Derek Black to interview him but Black initially refused. He moved across the country and changed his name. But a few months before the 2016 elections, Black sent Saslow an email which said he wanted to talk to him. They exchanged emails over the year discussing events in the country and in Europe, particularly the rise of nationalism in many countries. Saslow says Black realized that there is a real threat in what is happening in the country. Black also felt responsible for spreading racist views in the past which led to many deaths and general unrest. Saslow did an initial story about him in 2016 for the Washington Post. He realized that a 6,000-word story does not do justice to Black's story. He felt that there was more to be said. "His transformation was so huge and so profound that doing it in any short form almost hurts the believability," he says in an interview. Black went through a two to three-year transformation and it was a "tortured process." Saslow had to write a full-length book about his story to capture everything he went through. He had to earn Black's trust first before he could interview him. Balck was very cautious. He did not right away divulge his address and the real names of his friends who helped him go through the transformation. Saslow believes that Black still feels so much shame and embarrassment for the past things he did. He does not see the book as a positive and hopeful thing for him because of his feelings of shame. Interviewing Derek's family was more complicated than interviewing Derek's friends in college. His father Don was willing to be interviewed because it allowed him to know more about his son's situation. Saslow says Black's father is still very hurt about Derek's change of heart. They have stopped talking. "I think going through these times with me was a way of engaging with him in a way that he probably missed," says Saslow of Derek's father.

It was important for Saslow to show that Don Black loved and cared about his son because it was the truth. He wants the reader to understand that father and had a strong bond and that it was very difficult for Derek to break that bond. Saslow hopes that readers understand that Derek knew his conversion would crush the person who he always admired and loved. Saslow says it was hard for him to strike the balance in showing Don Black as a genuinely caring father and a white supremacist. In the end, "he still believes that his ideology is this righteous thing. He ends at the same place," Saslow says. He hopes he struck the balance he aimed for. Saslow has a Jewish father and a Christian mother. He grew up without religion. He admits that in the times he spent talking to Don he never really felt physically threatened. "He was always very curious about me," he says of the Derek Black's father.

Rising Out of Hatred is Saslow's second book. His first book, *Ten Letters: The Stories Americans Tell Their President* was published in 2012. He won the 2014 Pulitzer Prize for Explanatory Reporting. He was also a Pulitzer finalist in 2013, 2016, and 2017 for feature writing.

Bonus Downloads
Get Free Books with __Any Purchase__ of Conversation Starters!

Every purchase comes with a FREE download!

Add spice to any conversation
Never run out of things to say
Spend time with those you love

Get it Now

<u>or Click Here.</u>

Scan Your Phone

Fireside Questions

"What would you do?"

Tip: These questions can be a fun exercise as it spurs creativity among the readers by allowing alternate scene endings and "if this was you" questions.

~~~

question 21

Eli Saslow spent hundreds of hours talking to Derek Black in order to understand him and his conversion. He also interviewed his classmates at the New College in Florida, including those who refused to talk to him as well as those who engaged with him in discussions and debates. There were immigrant students and Jewish students who were also interviewed for the book. Saslow also interviewed people from the white nationalist movement, including Derek's family. He had access to Black's emails, g-chats, Facebook where Black held debates that promoted his racist beliefs. Why is it important to have a thorough research for the book? What is Saslow's intent in writing a well-detailed book about Black's conversion?

~~~

~ ~ ~

question 22

Saslow tried to reach Derek Black to interview him
but Black initially refused. He moved across the
country and changed his name. But a few months
before the 2016 elections, Black sent Saslow an
email which said he wanted to talk to him. They
exchanged emails over the year discussing events
in the country and in Europe, particularly the rise
of nationalism in many countries. Why did it take
long for Black to decide to talk to Saslow?

~ ~ ~

question 23

Saslow did an initial story about him in 2016 for the Washington Post. He realized that a 6,000-word story does not do justice to Black's story. He felt that there was more to be said. "His transformation was so huge and so profound that doing it in any short form almost hurts the believability," he says in an interview. Black went through a two to three-year transformation and it was a "tortured process." Saslow had to write a full-length book about his story to capture everything he went through. Do you think the book is exhaustive in detailing Black's conversion? Why? Why not?

~ ~ ~

question 24

Interviewing Derek's family was more complicated than interviewing Derek's friends in college. His father Don was willing to be interviewed because it allowed him to know more about his son's situation. Saslow says Black's father is still very hurt about Derek's change of heart. They have stopped talking. "I think going through these times with me was a way of engaging with him in a way that he probably missed," says Saslow of Derek's father. How does Saslow portray Derek's father? How do you feel about him based on Saslow's portrayal?

~~~

question 25

Rising Out of Hatred is Saslow's second book. His first book, Ten Letters: The Stories Americans Tell Their President was published in 2012. He won the 2014 Pulitzer Prize for Explanatory Reporting. He was also a Pulitzer finalist in 2013, 2016, and 2017 for feature writing. What was his Pulitzer Prize-winning story about?

~~~

~~~

question 26

Some students learned about his white supremacist ties and activities and exposed him resulting to his being shunned at school. Of the few people who attempted to befriend him, this included a Jewish student leader who invited him to Shabbat dinners at home with his Jewish family and a white girl who believed there is a nice person behind his racist veneer. His beliefs slowly changed. If none of these people extended their friendship to him do you think he would have converted? Why? Why not?

~~~

~~~

question 27

He realized that he needed to publicly express his new views about racism. He wrote a letter to the Southern Poverty Law Center and admitted his previously harmful actions that perpetuated racism against people of color and of Jewish descent. If he did not publicly express his change of heart, do you think he would still a converted person today? How important is his public expression?

~~~

question 28

Saslow shows how Black went through evasion and contradictions as he evolved in his views. He noted the talks between Black and Gornick which indicated how Black made small revisions to his beliefs, including his acknowledging that he respects people of different colors and that he is a white nationalist who needs to protect other whites as if they are an endangered species. Saslow notes the significant change in his beliefs. If Saslow did not detail the process of change he went through, how will it change your view of Black?

~~~

~~~

question 29

In writing his apology to the Southern Poverty Law Center, Black's words are quoted by Saslow: "It has become clear to me that white nationalism is not a movement of positive identity or of asserting cultural values…I can't support a movement that tells me I can't be a friend to whomever I wish or that other people's races require me to think about them in a certain way…" If Saslow did not quote Black, do you think the book will not be convincing enough? Why? Why not?

~~~

question 30

His father Don was willing to be interviewed because it allowed him to know more about his son's situation. Saslow says Black's father is still very hurt about Derek's change of heart. They have stopped talking. "I think going through these times with me was a way of engaging with him in a way that he probably missed," says Saslow of Derek's father. If Black's father did not allow the interviews with Saslow, how would the book have turned out?

~~~

Quiz Questions

"Ready to Announce the Winners?"

Tip: Create a leaderboard and track scores to see who gets the most correct answers. Winners required. Prizes optional.

~~~

quiz question 1

Derek Black's father is the founder of _____, the Internet's largest racist group.

~~~

quiz question 2

Black met _____, who used to shun him but gradually saw a different person behind his racist cloak. "She thought he seemed quirky, gentle, and interesting…" the author writes. Saslow features her as a prominent figure in Black's conversion.

~ ~ ~

~~~

quiz question 3

He believed that _____ was racist, and that James Monroe, Thomas Jefferson, and other historical leaders were similarly against people of color.

~~~

~~~

quiz question 4

True or False: He ran and won as committeeman in Palm Beach County, Florida using white victimhood for his platform.

~~~

~~~

quiz question 5

True or False: Saslow shows how Black went through evasion and contradictions as he evolved in his views. He noted the talks between Black and Gornick which indicated how Black made small revisions to his beliefs.

~~~

quiz question 6

True or False: A highlight in the book is one of the major turning points in his conversion. This is the time when he realized that his father's views have become unacceptable, like that of his support for George Zimmerman. Black was horrified also because it showed him "…a memory of his previous self" who made flawed arguments and expressed callousness, cruelty, and ignorance.

~~~

quiz question 7

True or False: He wrote a letter to Barack Obama and admitted his previously harmful actions that perpetuated racism against people of color and of Jewish descent.

~~~

quiz question 8

Rising Out of Hatred is Saslow's _____book. His first book, Ten Letters: The Stories Americans Tell Their President was published in 2012.

~~~

~~~

quiz question 9

He won the 2014 Pulitzer Prize for _____. He was also a Pulitzer finalist in 2013, 2016, and 2017 for feature writing.

~~~

~~~

quiz question 10

True or False: Saslow had to earn Black's trust first before he could interview him. Black was very cautious. He did not right away divulge his address and the real names of his friends who helped him go through the transformation.

~~~

quiz question 11

True or False: Saslow believes that Black still feels so much shame and embarrassment for the past things he did. Black does not see the book as a positive and hopeful thing for him because of his feelings of shame.

~~~

~~~

quiz question 12

True or False: Eli Saslow spent hundreds of hours talking to Derek Black in order to understand him and his conversion. He also interviewed his classmates at the New College in Florida, including those who refused to talk to him as well as those who engaged with him in discussions and debates. There were immigrant students and Jewish students who were also interviewed for the book.

~~~

Quiz Answers

1.   Stormfront
2.   Allison Gornick
3.   Abraham Lincoln
4.   True
5.   True
6.   True
7.   False
8.   second
9.   Explanatory Reporting
10.   True
11.   True
12.   True

Ways to Continue Your Reading

E VERY month, our team runs through a wide selection of books to pick the best titles for readers and reading groups, and promotes these titles to our thousands of readers – sometimes with free downloads, sale dates, and additional brochures.

Click here to sign up for these benefits.

If you have not yet read the original work or would like to read it again, you can purchase the original book here.

Bonus Downloads
*Get Free Books with **Any Purchase** of* Conversation Starters!

Every purchase comes with a FREE download!

Add spice to any conversation
Never run out of things to say
Spend time with those you love

Get it Now

or Click Here.

Scan Your Phone

On the Next Page…

If you found this book helpful to your discussions and rate it a 4 or 5, please write us a review on the next page.

Any length would be fine but we'd appreciate hearing you more! We'd be very encouraged.

Till next time,

BookHabits

"Loving Books is Actually a Habit"

CPSIA information can be obtained
at www.ICGtesting.com
Printed in the USA
LVHW041150180319
611004LV00006B/536/P